THE D.B. COOPER HIJACKING

VANISHING ACT

true crime

THE D.B. COOPER HIJACKING

VANISHING ACT

by Kay Melchisedech Olson

Content Advisers: Larry Carr, D.B. Cooper Case Agent,
Federal Bureau of Investigation, Seattle, Washington
Philip Edney, Public Affairs Specialist, Federal Bureau of
Investigation, Washington, D.C.

Reading Adviser: Alexa L. Sandmann, EdD,
Professor of Literacy, College and Graduate School
of Education, Health, and Human Services, Kent State University

COMPASS POINT BOOKS
a capstone imprint

Compass Point Books
151 Good Counsel Drive
P.O. Box 669
Mankato, MN 56002-0669

This book was manufactured with paper containing
at least 10 percent post-consumer waste.

Editor: Brenda Haugen
Designers: Tracy Davies and Gene Bentdahl
Media Researcher: Marcie Spence
Library Consultant: Kathleen Baxter
Production Specialist: Jane Klenk

Library of Congress Cataloging-in-Publication Data
Olson, Kay Melchisedech.
  The D.B. Cooper hijacking : vanishing act / by Kay Melchisedech Olson.
     p. cm. — (True crime)
  Includes bibliographical references and index.
  ISBN 978-0-7565-4359-4 (library binding)
  1. Cooper, D.B. 2. Hijacking of aircraft—United States—Case
studies. 3. Criminals—United States—Biography. I. Title. II. Series.
  HE9803.Z7H56 2011
  364.15'52092—dc22 [B]   2010006550

Image Credits: AP Images: cover (middle and top), 20, 23, 87, STF, 11,
Eric Risberg, 81; Bettmann/Corbis, 43, 53, 63; iStockphoto: bbossom, 2,
spaceprobe, cover (bottom); Melanie Conner/*The Oregonian*/Landov LLC,
29, 82; Sherlock Investigations, Inc., 56; Time Life Pictures/FBI/Getty
Images Inc., 32; Universal/The Kobal Collection, 78.

Visit Compass Point Books on the Internet at *www.capstonepub.com*

"I THINK IT'S A GREAT MYSTERY."

Few crimes are so shocking or so terrifying that the stories of what happened live on years, or even decades, after the offenses occurred. The shock waves from these crimes often ripple beyond the areas where they happened, fascinating and frightening entire nations—and sometimes the world. Some of these crimes are solved. Often they are not. But even when the cases grow cold, the evidence remains and awakens the amateur detective in all of us.

TABLE OF CONTENTS

CHAPTER

THE
SILENT
SETUP

Thanksgiving was just a day away. Most Americans were busy making preparations for food, family, and a break from their usual routines. Others, however, were hard at work. Some jobs, such as those in the travel industry, become more demanding during the holidays. Families come together for occasions such as Thanksgiving, and travel is part of many people's holiday plans.

A Northwest Orient Airlines Boeing 727 was shuttling people across the country that day, November 24, 1971. It had left Washington, D.C., in the morning. It stopped in Minneapolis, Minnesota, and then went to Montana, landing in Great Falls and Missoula. A stop in Spokane, Washington, was followed by another in Portland, Oregon. Here the airplane waited for its final flight of the day, to Seattle, Washington.

One person waiting in line to buy a ticket for Flight 305 was a neatly dressed man, probably in his mid-40s. He was fairly tall, between 5 feet 10 inches (178 centimeters) and 6 feet (183 cm). He weighed a trim 170 to 180 pounds (77 to 82 kilograms). He wore a dark suit, white shirt, and a black necktie with a mother-of-pearl tie tack. He had loafers on his feet and wore a black raincoat against the November chill. He probably raised no one's suspicions as he walked up to the Northwest ticket counter.

The man paid $20 cash for a seat in row 18 of the plane. He said his name was Dan Cooper, and he wasn't asked to show identification. He carried a briefcase but had no luggage to check.

Cooper boarded the plane and settled into his seat. He was the only passenger in row 18, the last row on the plane. Despite being the afternoon before Thanksgiving, the plane had only 36 passengers—less than half of its capacity. All indications were that the flight would be uneventful.

The same could not be said for all flights in those days. Hijackings were plentiful from 1968 through 1972. At least 326 were reported worldwide in that five-year span. Yet security was almost nonexistent then. Neither Cooper's nor any other passenger's carry-on bags were examined. Probably no one was thinking about a hijacking on this flight. No one, that is, except the man in row 18 who identified himself as Dan Cooper.

The crew of Northwest Orient Flight 305 included First Officer William Rataczak (left), Captain William Scott, and stewardess Tina Mucklow.

In the early 1970s, a female flight attendant was called a stewardess. Passengers expected stewardesses to be young, attractive, and attentive. Some men gave them unwelcome attention, made suggestive comments, or asked for dates. Cooper behaved like a gentleman. He politely asked for a drink—whiskey and 7UP—shortly after he boarded the plane.

As he waited for his drink, Cooper removed a pack of Raleigh cigarettes from his pocket. Drawing one from the pack, he lit it, inhaled, and slowly released the smoke into the air. No one protested. Separate sections of airplanes for nonsmokers would not appear until 1973, and totally smoke-free flights weren't available until the late 1980s.

While Cooper was smoking, stewardess Florence Schaffner brought him the drink he had ordered. He stared at her as he handed her a $20 bill. He told her to keep the change.

As the plane started taxiing down the runway to take off, Cooper handed Schaffner a note.

"MISS, YOU SHOULD READ THE NOTE I GAVE YOU."

She slipped the folded piece of paper into her pocket, but she wondered what it was. A love note? A suggestion that he would like to spend Thanksgiving with her? Perhaps the man in row 18 was not such a gentleman after all. She had received plenty of impolite offers from male passengers. This guy just put his in writing. She thought no more about it.

Schaffner was about to go on with her duties when she heard what Cooper said next.

"Miss, you should read the note I gave you," he said. "I have a bomb in my briefcase."

Did she hear him correctly? What did he say? Was this some kind of a joke? Was this average-looking man crazy? If he was kidding, this bomb-in-the-briefcase joke was not funny. She unfolded the note and read Cooper's message:

MISS. I have a bomb here and I would like you to sit by me.

Schaffner did as he asked and sat down. Cooper told her to write down his next words:

"I want $200,000 by 5:00 p.m. in cash. Put it in a knapsack. I want two back parachutes and two front parachutes. When we land, I want a fuel truck ready to refuel. No funny stuff, or I'll do the job."

Schaffner wrote the message as the man had demanded. Then he let her walk away.

"NO FUNNY STUFF, OR I'LL DO THE JOB."

CHAPTER

THE CRIME UNFOLDS

Florence Schaffner immediately showed the note with the man's demands to Tina Mucklow, another stewardess on Flight 305. They looked at each other, hoping it was a joke but fearing it was not. All sorts of thoughts raced through their minds. They quietly whispered back and forth.

"**CAN THIS REALLY BE HAPPENING?**"

"Do you think he's kidding?"

"Does he seem normal? I mean, do you think he's crazy?"

"Can this really be happening?"

"What should we do?"

After a brief moment of shared panic, they remembered the training they had received. They became calm and focused. Mucklow took the seat next to Cooper, where she remained for the rest of the flight. Schaffner took the note to the pilot, Captain William Scott. He read it, looked at the serious expression on Schaffner's face, and read the note again. Scott remained calm. He contacted Seattle-Tacoma air traffic control. The controllers there notified the Seattle police and the Federal Bureau of Investigation. The FBI contacted Northwest's president, Donald Nyrop. He sent a message telling Scott to cooperate with the hijacker.

While Flight 305 circled the Seattle airport before landing, a flurry of activity was going on below. Northwest arranged to borrow the money Cooper demanded from SeaFirst Bank in Seattle. Like most large banks, SeaFirst had money set aside for such events. Officials at the bank already had photos of all of the bills. If a criminal tried to spend it, police would know it had been stolen.

While the parachutes Cooper had demanded were being prepared, authorities wondered why he wanted two sets of chutes. Was one of the passengers on board an accomplice of Cooper's? Was he planning to force one of the crew members to jump with him? Or was it a way to make sure the chutes would be safe? If the authorities suspected that a crew member would be forced to jump with Cooper, they wouldn't disable the parachutes.

The pilot kept circling the airport, stalling for time until Cooper's demands could be met. The plane's passengers, who didn't know what was going on, were sure to question why the landing was being delayed. The captain talked to them over the intercom:

"This is Captain Scott in the cockpit, folks. It looks like the ground crew is pretty busy tonight. We are waiting for a runway to be cleared for landing. In

"... WE'LL GET YOU SAFELY ON THE GROUND JUST AS SOON AS POSSIBLE."

the meantime, sit back, relax, and we'll get you safely on the ground just as soon as possible."

Finally, at 5:24 p.m., air traffic control radioed Scott. Cooper's demands had been met. At 5:40 p.m., the plane landed, but it did not move to a terminal gate. Instead the plane taxied to an

The hijacked airplane sat on the runway in Seattle, illuminated by bright floodlights.

area lighted by floodlights. Once again the pilot spoke to the passengers.

"Ah, folks, this is the captain again," Scott said over the intercom. "We're going to have to ask you to remain seated with your seatbelts fastened for just a moment or two. We'll get you on your way just as soon as we can, and we thank you for your patience."

Portable stairs were driven to the front of the airplane. Stewardess Mucklow made several trips out of the airplane to get the money and parachutes Cooper had demanded.

Mucklow was a tall woman with light brown hair that she wore pulled back with a yellow ribbon. Her calmness masked the nervousness she felt as she went up and down the stairs carrying the money and the parachutes. She was sure no one could miss her thumping heartbeat and trembling hands. Although passengers were annoyed with the delay, they still seemed unaware of the hijacking.

After retrieving the items, Mucklow brought them to Cooper. He nodded his approval.

"What about the passengers?" she asked Cooper. "They're bound to start suspecting something is wrong."

Cooper told her

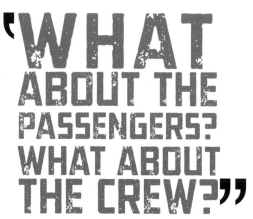

that the passengers could leave by the portable stairs.

"What about the crew?" she asked.

"You and the flight crew stay. Everyone else can go, but do it quickly," he said.

The 36 passengers and stewardess Florence Schaffner left the plane. Mucklow, Scott, and the other two members of the flight crew stayed on board with Cooper.

As the plane was being refueled, Cooper inspected the money and parachutes. Satisfied that his demands had been met, he told Mucklow to instruct the pilot to take off and fly toward Mexico.

The plane carried 36 passengers and crew. Most of the people on the flight didn't realize that it had been hijacked.

"I DON'T WANT TO JUMP OUT OF THE PLANE ..."

Mexico? Mucklow wondered whether she would be spending Thanksgiving so far from home.

Returning from the cockpit a few moments later, she relayed a message to Cooper. "The captain says that Mexico is out of range unless we stop in Reno to refuel." Cooper took a drag on his cigarette and thought for a moment. "Fine," he said.

Mucklow returned to the cockpit to relay Cooper's answer.

With the plane flying toward Reno, a city in western Nevada, Mucklow returned to Cooper's seat. She looked outside and noticed that the weather was getting worse. The plane was flying a low-altitude route that passed west of the Cascade

Mountains. A mix of cold November rain, snow, and sleet was falling. She saw that Cooper was using a pocket knife to cut a long piece of cord from one of the chutes. Suddenly she was filled with dread. He had two sets of front and back chutes. "Oh, no," she thought. "He's not going to make someone jump with him, is he? I don't want to jump out of the plane, especially in a storm like this."

Cooper stood up and gave Mucklow his final order. "Go back to the cockpit and stay there," he said in a matter-of-fact way.

Mucklow hurried back to the cockpit, happy to be away from Cooper if he was planning to jump.

"I don't think we're going to Mexico," Mucklow told the cockpit crew. "I think he's planning to use one of those parachutes to jump from the plane."

Could he be crazy enough, Captain Scott wondered, to try a stunt like that in this kind of weather? Using the intercom, he asked Cooper whether he needed help with anything.

"No!" was Cooper's firm reply.

THE COOPER VANE

Three similar hijackings were attempted after Cooper's 1971 escapade. The Boeing 727 was the only U.S. commercial airliner that had aft stairs. The Federal Aviation Administration decided something had to be done to prevent any more hijackers from using the plane's rear stairs as a jumping-off point. The FAA required that all 727s be fitted with a mechanical aerodynamic wedge. The wedge prevented the rear stairs from being lowered while the plane was in flight. The device was known as the Cooper Vane.

Cooper made his way to the back of the plane. He used the parachute cord he had cut to tie the bag of money tightly around his waist. He opened the plane's rear door and lowered the stairs as freezing air filled the doorway. The crew noticed their ears popping, a sign of an air pressure change in the cabin. Then they felt a bump, which apparently came from the back stairway.

Cooper had jumped from the back stairs and was falling to the ground through a heavy rain and sleet storm. He was wearing the same clothes—minus the necktie, which he had removed—that he had had on when he boarded the plane. Was he carrying the briefcase that held a supposed bomb, or had he tossed it away? Real or not, the bomb threat had done its job in carrying out the hijacking. Cooper now had to hope the parachute would do its job in his getaway.

CHAPTER

FEW
CLUES

W ith the hijacker gone, the plane flew to the Reno airport. The landing was uneventful. The 727 was immediately surrounded by FBI agents and police. They wasted no time hunting for clues. Unfortunately there were few to find.

Cooper left behind his tie and tie tack and two of the four parachutes. Agents found fingerprints, but they didn't know whether they belonged to Cooper. Saliva on the whiskey glass and cigarette butts was of little use. Identification through DNA was still decades in the future.

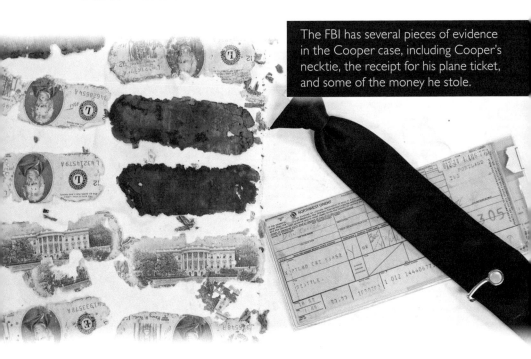

The FBI has several pieces of evidence in the Cooper case, including Cooper's necktie, the receipt for his plane ticket, and some of the money he stole.

Cooper's briefcase and a placard showing how to lower the plane's back stairs were missing. Cooper probably either threw them out of the plane or held onto them as he jumped. Other than his tie and tie tack, Cooper left no clothes behind. Agents knew he was not properly dressed for the cold and rainy November weather. If he landed in the mountains, his raincoat and loafers, if he still had them, were hardly what he needed for hiking in rugged terrain.

The crew members and passengers helped an artist create a composite sketch of Cooper. Soon the likeness of this very ordinary-looking man was all over the news. One news reporter mistakenly identified the hijacker as D.B. Cooper, even though he had given the name Dan Cooper at the Northwest ticket counter. The mistake stuck. Although the FBI gave the case the code name NORJAK, for Northwest hijacking, it has always been called the case of D.B. Cooper.

Undaunted by the scarcity of clues Cooper left behind, authorities began ground searches for the

WHY THE NAME DAN COOPER?

The NORJAK hijacker's use of the name Dan Cooper is puzzling. Some people believe the hijacker may have enjoyed reading the adventures of a comic book character named Dan Cooper. The comic book was popular in France in the 1960s and early 1970s. An issue published before the NORJAK caper showed the Dan Cooper character parachuting out of an airplane.

The Cooper investigation remains open. FBI agent Larry Carr, who is handling leads in the investigation, thinks the comic character might have something to do with the case. The Dan Cooper comics were never translated into English. Carr thinks the hijacker may have served in the U.S. Air Force and spent time in Europe. He could have come across the Dan Cooper comics there and used the name in the hijacking.

A composite sketch of Cooper was created from eyewitness descriptions. Because he looked so clean-cut and ordinary, other passengers on the plane didn't suspect he was causing any trouble.

hijacker. A composite sketch, based on eyewitness descriptions, remains the only likeness of the man known as D.B. Cooper. FBI agents feel confident that the sketch is accurate because it is based on nearly identical descriptions given by people questioned individually.

They are much less confident about where Cooper landed. Because of the varying winds, an exact landing spot was impossible to determine based on the plane's speed and altitude. That fact was both good and bad for the searchers looking for Cooper. Good because it means the hijacker probably did not have an accomplice waiting on the ground. Bad because the search area was extensive.

Searchers began looking at a 28-square-mile (73-square-kilometer) area south of Lake Merwin near Ariel, Washington. FBI agents and sheriff's deputies searched the area with helicopters, on foot over rugged terrain, and with patrol boats on Lake Merwin and nearby Yale Lake. No trace of Cooper, the loot, or the briefcase was found.

With the spring thaw in early 1972, the search began anew. This time FBI agents were joined by 200 U.S. Army troops from Fort Lewis in Tacoma, Washington. Air Force pilots, National Guard troops, and civilian volunteers joined in the hunt. They searched the area for 18 straight days in March and another 18 straight days in April. It was one of the most intense manhunts in the Pacific Northwest. Yet it yielded absolutely no evidence.

Had Cooper made a clean getaway after landing, or were searchers looking in the wrong place?

THE D.B. COOPER PARTY

During the manhunt for D.B. Cooper in the 1970s, the tiny town of Ariel, Washington, became an unofficial headquarters for searchers. In 1974, and every year since, the town has held a D.B. Cooper Party at the Ariel Store and Tavern.

Festivities are held the Saturday after Thanksgiving. The party starts about 1:00 p.m. and lasts until about midnight. Some years there are story-telling contests. Sometimes there are D.B. Cooper look-alike contests. Mostly folks hang around listening to music and remembering the infamous unsolved hijacking.

Store owner Dona Elliott still remembers the night in 1971 when it all started. She was baking pumpkin pies and heard a jet's engines. "It was flying so low and it was raining," she recalls. "I said, 'Wow, that plane is gonna crash.'"

The plane didn't crash, of course, and Elliott doesn't think Cooper did, either. "I just think he was ticked off with the government and wanted to get away with something," Elliott says. "And he has—so far."

CHAPTER

4

COPYCAT?

A lthough ground and air searches
failed to discover D.B. Cooper's
landing site, FBI agents lost no
time investigating likely suspects. But soon their
attention was drawn elsewhere. On April 7, 1972,
while searchers were still looking for Cooper on the
ground, another airplane was hijacked.

United Airlines Flight 855 was flying from
Newark, New Jersey, to Los Angeles, California.
The Boeing 727 had 85 passengers aboard with
a flight crew of six. After a stopover in Denver,
Colorado, the plane was once again airborne. About
20 minutes into this leg of the journey, a passenger
noticed a man holding what looked like a hand
grenade and reported it to a stewardess.

She immediately informed the pilot, who
devised a plan to calmly check out the situation. He
asked an off-duty pilot, who was aboard the plane
as a passenger, to walk casually by the man to see
whether he was really holding a hand grenade. But
as the off-duty pilot did so, the passenger drew a

gun and handed the off-duty pilot a sealed envelope labeled "hijack instructions." He insisted that a stewardess deliver the envelope to the pilot.

The crew and the off-duty pilot acted so calmly that few passengers knew that anything was wrong. Using the intercom, the pilot announced that the plane had a minor mechanical problem and he would make an unscheduled landing in Grand Junction, Colorado.

The hijacking note was typed on two sheets of paper. Also in the envelope were a bullet and the pin from a hand grenade. The pin is a safety device that keeps the grenade from exploding. These items were probably put in the envelope to show that the hijacker was serious.

The note told the pilot to fly to a San Francisco airport and park at runway 19. The hijacker demanded $500,000 in cash, four parachutes, and the return of the note.

The cockpit crew looked at one another. These demands sounded very similar to those made in

"WE APOLOGIZE FOR THE INCONVENIENCE, BUT YOUR SAFETY IS OUR MAIN CONCERN."

the Cooper hijacking a few months earlier. Could this be the same guy? Was he attempting to pull off a second hijacking? It was impossible to know, but the crew was certain that the hand-grenade-holding passenger was no one to fool with. The pilot turned the plane on a course toward San Francisco.

The pilot explained the course change to the passengers: "Folks, this is the captain again. It seems that Grand Junction isn't able to handle our repairs, so we are instead going to land in San

Francisco. We apologize for the inconvenience, but your safety is our main concern."

The safety of Flight 855 was, indeed, the main concern of United Airlines officials. After the plane landed in San Francisco, they delivered two bags loaded with cash, along with the four parachutes. Unlike D.B. Cooper, this hijacker had checked his luggage on the flight. He demanded that it be brought to him from the baggage compartment.

With his demands met and the plane refueled, the hijacker allowed the passengers and one stewardess to leave the plane. He ordered that the cockpit crew and another stewardess—who was kept busy relaying notes between the hijacker and the pilot—stay aboard.

The pilot was instructed to fly at an altitude of 16,000 feet (5,000 meters) at a speed of 200 miles (322 km) per hour. He was to follow a flight course over Utah. The hijacker threatened to use explosives to blow up the plane after jumping if pursuit planes followed the airliner.

There were as many differences as similarities between Cooper's caper and this hijacking. Some differences were improvements. This hijacker had packed a suitcase with a jumpsuit and a helmet, which he put on before jumping with the parachute. Had Cooper learned a cold and bitter lesson when he jumped during the November storm?

Whether or not he was Cooper, this hijacker also jumped from the 727's rear stairs. The flight crew then headed for the airport in Salt Lake City, where it was met by FBI agents.

This time more clues had been left behind. Agents collected just about anything the hijacker may have touched—seat belts, gum wrappers, cigarette butts, and a hand-printed note he left behind. Crew members and passengers were carefully questioned about what they had observed.

A search began in an area near Provo, Utah, where it was estimated the hijacker jumped. A sheriff's posse, FBI agents, and police scoured the countryside looking for the hijacker or evidence of his jump. They found nothing, but they soon had a promising lead—a tip from a concerned citizen.

Agents heard from an acquaintance of Richard Floyd McCoy Jr. According to the tip, McCoy, before the hijacking, had bragged about a foolproof plan for hijacking an airplane.

McCoy had serious financial problems and seemed to have the background of a hijacker. He was a Vietnam War veteran, a helicopter pilot, and a skydiver. He was said to be a member of the Utah Air National Guard.

FBI agents found that McCoy's handwriting matched the writing in the note that the hijacker had left on the plane. Someone who was shown McCoy's picture said he looked like a man he had seen asking for a ride near Provo the night of the crime.

A search of McCoy's home turned up $499,970 in cash—a few dollars short of the ransom amount. McCoy was arrested, tried, and sentenced to 45 years in prison. His story did not end at the federal penitentiary in Lewisburg, Pennsylvania, however.

Richard Floyd McCoy Jr. was escorted by federal officials after being charged with hijacking United Airlines Flight 855. McCoy was captured near his home in Provo, Utah, near Brigham Young University, where he was a junior studying law enforcement.

"WHEN I SHOT RICHARD MCCOY, I SHOT D.B. COOPER at the SAME TIME."

In 1974 McCoy made a gun and escaped with a fellow prison inmate. They stole a garbage truck, crashed through a gate, and made their getaway.

Three months later FBI agents found McCoy in Virginia, and he fired at them with a pistol. Agent Nicholas O'Hara fired back, killing McCoy. O'Hara believed McCoy and Cooper were the same person.

"When I shot Richard McCoy, I shot D.B. Cooper at the same time," O'Hara said.

McCoy didn't admit that he was Cooper, but he didn't say he wasn't, either. He simply said, "I don't want to talk to you about it."

However, unlike O'Hara, not everyone in the FBI was convinced that McCoy was Cooper. Through the years, other possible suspects also have emerged, and the case remains open.

CHAPTER 5

DEATHBED
CONFESSION?

About seven years after the Cooper hijacking, Duane Weber and his bride, Jo, were married. Weber had never told Jo anything about his life before he had met her. He had just said that his life began with her, and she didn't ask questions about his past. But much of his behavior puzzled her.

Soon after their wedding, Weber had a nightmare and began to talk in his sleep. He said something about leaving fingerprints on the "aft stairs." Jo had no idea what he was talking about and wasn't sure she had heard him correctly. She certainly didn't connect his sleep talking with D.B. Cooper's jump from the rear stairs of a 727. Still she remembers that he woke dripping with sweat and quite shaken.

Weber had plenty of reasons to have bad dreams. Although he had told his wife his life had begun with her, he did have a shady past. He had been married several times before marrying Jo. He had served in the Army and gotten a bad-conduct discharge from the Navy. Using the name John C. Collins, he had committed burglary and forgery. He served time in the Missouri State Penitentiary and five other prisons from 1945 to 1968. Other secrets he kept well-hidden, but it was clear to Jo that something nagged at his conscience now and then.

A decade and a half after their marriage, Weber had settled into a comfortable, law-abiding life with Jo. They lived in Florida, and Weber made his living as an antiques dealer. But their life together was ending. In early 1995 Weber had kidney disease and was close to death in a Pensacola hospital. As Jo sat by her husband's hospital bed, he motioned for her to come closer.

"I'm Dan Cooper," he whispered.

Was he making a dying confession? Jo had no idea what he meant. Maybe he was talking in his sleep again. Maybe pain medication was making him hallucinate. She didn't connect his words with the 1971 Cooper hijacking. Weber died 11 days later without revealing any more of his mysterious past.

"DID YOU EVER THINK HE MIGHT BE D.B. COOPER?"

After her husband's death, Jo sold his van. The new owner found—and returned—a wallet stashed inside the vehicle. The wallet contained Weber's bad-conduct discharge. It also held a Social Security card and a prison-release form, both of which bore the name John C. Collins.

Jo began thinking a bit more about her husband's life before their marriage. She talked to a friend about things that puzzled her. Weber had suffered a knee injury before meeting her. He said it had happened when he had jumped out of a plane. In 1979, while on vacation, Weber took a walk by himself near the Columbia River. Four months later a young boy found a bunch of rotting $20 bills from the D.B. Cooper hijacking in almost the same spot where Weber had been.

"Did you ever think he might be D.B. Cooper?" the friend asked Jo.

Wanting to know more, Jo began doing some of her own investigating. She went to a library and checked out a book about D.B. Cooper. It was the first time she had realized that the hijacker had used the name Dan Cooper instead of D.B. Cooper. It was curious that Weber had whispered, as he lay dying, that he was Dan Cooper and not D.B. Cooper.

Curious, too, were some penciled notes in the margins of the library book. Jo didn't remember that her husband had ever gone to the library, but the notes seemed to be written in her husband's handwriting. The book's descriptions of Cooper also seemed to match Weber as he probably would have looked in 1971.

Jo remembered more coincidences. She had found a white bank bag stashed in a cooler Weber kept in his van. The NORJAK ransom money had been delivered to Cooper in a white canvas bank bag. Going over tax records while her husband was still alive, Jo had found an old Northwest Orient Airlines plane ticket stub with the destination "SEA-TAC," the abbreviation for the Seattle-Tacoma airport. When she looked for it after Weber's death, however, the ticket had disappeared.

Besides saying that he was Dan Cooper, Weber had said something else as he was dying in the hospital. Jo and Anne Faass, a former employee of the couple, were at Weber's side when he began

"... HE SURE DID SEND ME ON THE WILDEST RIDE ANY WIDOW HAS EVER BEEN ON."

mumbling that he had forgotten where he buried $173,000 in a bucket. At the time they dismissed his ramblings as the side effects of pain medication. Later Jo gave it more thought. She began to believe that Weber just might have been Cooper.

She shared her hunch with the FBI, but agents showed little interest. Eventually Jo contacted former FBI agent Ralph Himmelsbach, who, until his retirement, had been in charge of the Cooper case. Himmelsbach urged the FBI to check out Weber as a possible NORJAK suspect. A file on Duane Weber was opened in March 1997. Agents interviewed Jo, Weber's brother, and one of his former wives. Weber's fingerprints were compared with the unidentified prints found on Flight 305, but none matched.

The circumstantial evidence against Weber is strong but not nearly strong enough to make a solid case. Himmelsbach believes the similarities between Weber and Cooper are enough to "stretch the imagination." Weber was eventually ruled out as a suspect because of DNA testing of the tie Cooper left behind. But Jo Weber is convinced that her husband was D.B. Cooper. "If he is not," she has said, "he sure did send me on the wildest ride any widow has ever been on."

FBI agent Ralph Himmelsbach (second from right) led the NORJAK investigation for about 10 years, but his interest in the case remained even beyond his retirement.

CHAPTER

DEAD
RINGER

In the early 1970s, Northwest Orient Airlines employee Kenneth Christiansen was living in the Seattle suburb of Bonney Lake, Washington. He had bought a house there just a few months after the D.B. Cooper hijacking. Some people thought it was curious that he could afford to pay $16,000 in cash for the property on his relatively low salary. It was curious, too, that he drank the same brand of liquor that Cooper did, smoked the same brand of cigarettes, and looked a lot like the eyewitness descriptions of Cooper.

As he was dying in 1994, Christiansen told his family that he had a big secret. He said he couldn't reveal the secret because he was afraid it would cause them a lot of trouble. He took the secret to his grave. Even so, no one then voiced suspicions that Christiansen might have been the NORJAK hijacker.

Several years later, though, Ken's brother Lyle suddenly made the connection. Lyle was watching an episode of *Unsolved Mysteries* on television that

Ken Christiansen never said he was D.B. Cooper. However, several people, including his brother, believe he probably was.

featured the 1971 hijacking. "My brother was a dead ringer to the composite sketch of D.B.," he said.

Lyle told the FBI about his suspicions. Ken had served as a paratrooper in the Army and had made many jumps from airplanes. His training included skydiving with up to 90 pounds (41 kg) of equipment strapped to his body. The ransom cash from the Cooper hijacking weighed only about 21 pounds (10 kg), which would have been an easy load for an experienced skydiver like Ken.

"I THINK YOU MIGHT BE ONTO SOMETHING HERE."

As a Northwest Orient employee, Ken would have been familiar with the Boeing 727 and its rear stairway. Besides, Lyle insisted, Ken looked just like the composite sketch of Cooper shown on the television program.

Florence Schaffner, one of the stewardesses on Cooper's flight, was inclined to agree. When shown a picture of Ken Christiansen, Schaffner said, "I think you might be onto something here."

The FBI did not agree. Ken was about 4 inches (10 centimeters) shorter and about 30 pounds (14 kg) lighter than Cooper, according to eyewitnesses. Also, Cooper was said to have brown eyes, and Ken's eyes were described as hazel.

The differences between eyewitness descriptions of D.B. Cooper and Ken Christiansen may not be great enough to rule him out as a suspect, however. Hazel eyes are light brown or strong yellowish brown. A witness might have mistakenly described hazel eyes as brown. And the differences of 30 pounds and 4 inches might not be important when considering that witnesses were estimating the weight and height of the hijacker.

Lyle Christiansen is convinced that his brother was D.B. Cooper. The FBI has released no information about whether Ken Christiansen has been identified or eliminated as a suspect in the NORJAK case.

CHAPTER

SUSPICIOUS
SON

D id William Pratt Gossett, a former military man who later became a priest, harbor a deep, dark secret that he took to the grave? Like other possible D.B. Cooper suspects, he had parachuting experience. While in the military, Gossett served in both Korea and Vietnam.

One of Gossett's three sons, Greg, remembers that his father had an addiction to gambling and always seemed to be short of money. An exception was at Christmas 1971, when, Greg says, his father had "wads" of cash. Greg thinks it was strange that a gambler who was always short of money would suddenly have lots of it just a few weeks after the Cooper hijacking.

Greg says his father, if he was the hijacker, may have stored some of the ransom money in a safe deposit box in Vancouver, British Columbia. He thinks a lot of it could have been gambled away in Las Vegas, Nevada, although no $20 bills bearing

"HE WALKED INTO MY OFFICE AND CLOSED THE DOOR AND SAID HE THOUGHT HE MIGHT BE IN SOME TROUBLE ..."

the ransom money's serial numbers have ever been found in circulation.

Greg also says that his father confessed to him, Gossett's other two sons, and other people that he actually was D.B. Cooper, the NORJAK hijacker.

Galen Cook, an attorney, is investigating Gossett's background for a book he intends to write about the Cooper case. He suggests that Gossett, who died in 2003, told several people, including one of his ex-wives, that he was the hijacker. Cook says a retired judge in Salt Lake City, Utah, listened as Gossett admitted to him in 1977 that he was Cooper.

Stewardess Florence Schaffner got a good look at D.B. Cooper when she served him a drink and sat next to him on the hijacked plane.

"He walked into my office and closed the door and said he thought he might be in some trouble, that he was involved in a hijacking in Portland and Seattle a few years ago and that he might have left prints behind," the retired judge told Cook. The judge said he advised Gossett to keep his mouth shut and not do anything stupid.

Cook's investigation into Gossett's background has uncovered some interesting facts. At one time in his life, Gossett worked as a private detective and specialized in cases of money fraud, cults, and missing persons. In 1988 he was ordained a priest in the Old Catholic Church and changed his name to Wolfgang. The Old Catholic Church differs from the Roman Catholic Church in its views regarding the pope, the spiritual leader of the world's 1 billion Catholics. Unlike members of the Roman Catholic

Church, members of the Old Catholic Church do not believe the pope is always correct.

Cook believes Gossett survived the stormy dive from the plane in 1971. Cook thinks he avoided searchers because he landed in Oregon instead of Washington. Gossett planned the hijacking with military precision, Cook says, and was able to return home to Utah three days later.

Cook gave the FBI a sample of Gossett's fingerprints. The FBI has not said whether the sample rules Gossett in or out of the D.B. Cooper suspect pool.

CHAPTER

DUAL
IDENTITY?

W hile the eyewitness descriptions of the NORJAK hijacker have varied slightly—height, weight, eye and hair color, and clothing—one physical trait has never changed. D.B. Cooper has always been described as a white man.

But what if he wasn't a man? What if he was a woman posing as a man?

Ron and Pat Forman, a married couple living in Washington state, have long been small-plane

Pat and Ron Forman and their Cessna 140

enthusiasts. In 1977, while visiting what is now Pierce County Airport near Puyallup, Washington, they met Barbara Dayton. She owned a Cessna 140, a single-engine, two-seat airplane, and she showed them another Cessna 140, parked next to hers, that was for sale. The Formans bought the plane and eventually became good friends with Dayton.

The Formans' new friend had unusual skills for a middle-aged woman in the 1970s. Dayton was an excellent pilot and an exceptional mechanic, and she knew a lot about electronics. Ron noticed that she ate more like a man than a woman. And it was hard to miss her masculine tattoos—a devil riding on a motorcycle, a black panther, and an arm's length of ports of call from her days in the merchant marine. Little of what the Formans observed about Dayton seemed to fit what they knew about their new friend, who worked as a librarian and spent her free time repairing and flying a small airplane.

When Dayton became more comfortable with the Formans, she shared her secret. After living for 43 years as Robert E. "Bobby" Dayton, she underwent a sex change operation in 1969 and became Barbara E. "Barb" Dayton.

Knowing Dayton's secret didn't change the Formans' affection for her, and their friendship

BOBBY   BARB

continued. The three often enjoyed the company of other amateur pilots around the Thun Field airstrip.

The subject of D.B. Cooper and the 1971 hijacking was a popular topic in the Seattle area at the time. Amateur pilots, sitting around sipping coffee and sharing stories, often speculated about the infamous crime.

The Formans soon noticed that their friend Dayton became upset when anyone made unfavorable comments about Cooper. She seemed to know more about the hijacking than the average small-plane pilot.

One day Dayton shared her version of how Cooper probably carried out the hijacking. She suggested that he used his own small plane to scout the landing area beforehand. She said that he chose the 727 because he knew the rear stairs would give him a safe departure point. She believed that he didn't just jump off blindly and land in the mountains, as the FBI had speculated. She explained that he would have used the lights of the

WHO IS D.B. COOPER?

Person	Background	Reasons to Believe	Reasons to Doubt
Richard McCoy	Served in the Vietnam War as a Green Beret helicopter pilot and was an avid skydiver	Committed a similar hijacking four months after the D.B. Cooper caper	When captured by the FBI, never admitted being Cooper
Kenneth Christiansen	Worked for Northwest Orient Airlines; had been a paratrooper	Brother says he fits the profile; before dying in 1994, Ken said, "There is something you should know, but I cannot tell you."	Eyewitness Florence Schaffner could not positively identify his photo
Duane Weber	Antiques dealer; discharged from U.S. Navy for bad conduct; served time in Missouri State Penitentiary	Before dying in 1995, confessed to his wife, "I'm Dan Cooper."	His fingerprints didn't match any of the prints taken inside the hijacked plane; a DNA test ruled him out
William Pratt "Wolfgang" Gossett	Served in the military, in Korea and Vietnam; was a survivalist and an experienced parachutist	Often spoke of the D.B. Cooper hijacking; told his sons, a retired judge, and a friend he was Cooper; was often in debt because of a gambling problem	The FBI hasn't said fingerprints have ruled Gossett out
Robert / Barbara Dayton	Had a sex-change operation (male to female) two years before the hijacking and may have acted like a man during the hijacking to fool authorities	Gave detailed information to friends about the hijacking; indicated the FBI had looked in the wrong area for Cooper's landing; was a pilot and had skydiving experience	Dayton's friends, Pat and Ron Forman, discussed their theory with the FBI, but the FBI has never commented on this person

"I AM D.B. COOPER."

cities below to help time his jump. Thus he would have been able to land safely near a predetermined spot where he had left a car and a change of clothes.

Dayton's detailed description left the Formans spellbound. How could she seem so sure of so many of the hijacking's details? When neither Ron nor Pat said anything, Dayton finally confessed. "I am D.B. Cooper," she said.

Several weeks later, Dayton gave the Formans more details about her supposed parachute-jump escape from the hijacked Northwest plane. She described how the ransom money bags had been tied around her waist and where she had hidden the loot—in a deserted water tank in an orchard.

The reason Dayton gave for committing the hijacking was as unconventional as she was.

Although she maintained that the dynamite in the briefcase was real, she had never intended to hurt anyone, she said. Most surprising of all, Dayton said she never had intended to spend the money. She was angry with the airlines and the Federal Aviation Administration. She wanted to be a professional pilot, but their many rules and conditions kept her from qualifying.

She also was bitter about being a female born in a male body. The Formans say she told them she chose the dangerous hijacking stunt as a way to get back at society.

Dayton died February 20, 2002, at the age of 76. It was then that the Formans began checking out the amazing stories their friend had shared with them. To their surprise, they found many of her far-fetched tales to be true. They began to believe that Dayton had become a woman and disguised herself as a man to carry out the hijacking. Barbara Dayton actually was the infamous D.B. Cooper, they believed.

"BY THE TIME WE FINISHED THE BOOK, WE WERE 98 PERCENT SURE."

The Formans have written a book about their friend and the D.B. Cooper case. When they started the book, they said, they were not totally convinced that Dayton was Cooper.

"By the time we finished the book, we were 98 percent sure," they wrote.

Continued research after the book was finished "has erased any possible doubt in our minds," they added. The FBI has declined to comment on whether she is a suspect.

CHAPTER

THE CASE
CONTINUES

Money is the motive for many crimes. The D.B. Cooper hijacking seemed to be no exception. Cooper had demanded, and received, 10,000 $20 bills. He took the money with him when he jumped off the stairway of the Boeing 727. If Cooper survived and still had the money, he probably would have begun spending it. With microfilm photos of the bills and a list of their serial numbers, all FBI agents had to do was follow the money trail.

But the money trail never started. If Cooper was still alive, he wasn't spending the cash. Why risk his life, and going to prison, for $200,000 if he wasn't going to spend any of it? FBI agents searched as hard for the cash as for Cooper himself. Agents alerted banks, savings and loan companies, and even Scotland Yard to the serial numbers of the ransom money. Northwest Orient Airlines offered a reward for recovery of the money. After several years passed and none of the cash surfaced, the

THE PURSUIT OF D.B. COOPER

The film *The Pursuit of D.B. Cooper* made its debut in 1981. Starring Treat Williams as Cooper, the movie is a fictional account of the hijacking. Most of the film speculates about what could have happened if Cooper had survived his jump from the plane and lived to enjoy his infamous exploit.

To get publicity for the movie, Universal Pictures put up a $1 million reward for information leading to the hijacker's capture. Nobody was ever able to claim the reward.

reward was canceled. The *Oregon Journal*, a Portland newspaper, published the serial numbers of the money and offered $1,000 to the first person to find a single $20 bill from the ransom. No one ever claimed the prize.

On February 10, 1980, an 8-year-old boy was enjoying a picnic with his family on the banks of the Columbia River near Vancouver, Washington. He began exploring and poking around by the water's edge. Young Brian Ingram was about to uncover a buried treasure. He spied three stacks of tattered $20 bills held together with rubber bands under a thin layer of sand. The bills were moldy and starting to deteriorate, but the serial numbers were readable.

Brian's father contacted the FBI with the find. There were 294 $20 bills ($5,880), and the money was soon identified as being part of the Cooper ransom. Now the mystery became even more complicated. Where was the rest of the loot—$194,120, to be exact? How long had the money Brian found been there?

FBI agent Ralph Himmelsbach didn't believe the money Brian found had been there since Cooper's 1971 hijacking. He didn't think the rubber bands around the recovered money would have survived in the elements for the nine years since Cooper's jump. So where had the money been before it was found on the bank of the Columbia? Why was some of the money found while the rest remained missing?

The FBI turned to scientific experts for help. Some theorized that the money Brian found had washed up on the beach after a dredging operation in 1974 by the Army Corps of Engineers. Others disagreed, citing the fact that the money was found above the clay deposited on the shoreline as a result of the dredge. Still others believed that the bills Brian found had washed into the Columbia River from the Washougal River, which was near Cooper's suspected landing area.

Nothing has ever been proved about the recovered money or the amount still missing. Brian Ingram was allowed to keep some of the money

Though the money found by Brian Ingram was badly deteriorated, many of the bills still showed their serial numbers in the lower left-hand corner. This helped the FBI determine it was part of the loot stolen by Cooper.

he found. He kept the weather-beaten bills as an heirloom for many years. In 2009, however, he sold some of the money at auction.

Although the NORJAK case has never been solved, many theories have been suggested to explain what happened to D.B. Cooper. The FBI

FBI agent Larry Carr continues to search for answers in the Cooper case. Among the evidence he has inherited is one of the parachutes Cooper had demanded.

believes it's doubtful that Cooper survived his jump from the Boeing 727. His loafers would have blown off during the jump, and it's unlikely that he could have hiked barefoot in rough terrain during a rainy November night. Some agents doubt that Cooper even managed to open the parachute.

Seattle FBI agent Larry Carr says, "We originally thought Cooper was an experienced jumper, perhaps even a paratrooper. We concluded after a few years this was simply not true. No experienced parachutist would have jumped in the pitch-black night, in the rain, with a 200-mile-an-hour wind in his face, wearing loafers and a trench coat. It was simply too risky. He also missed that his reserve chute was only for training and had been sewn shut—something a skilled skydiver would have checked."

Former FBI agent Richard Tosaw believes Cooper's skeleton can be found at the bottom of the Columbia River. Tosaw was so convinced that Cooper's jump ended in a splash that he conducted searches with scuba divers and grappling hooks in the river near where Brian Ingram found some of the ransom money. Although he found no evidence of Cooper, Tosaw is still sure that the river is the hijacker's final resting place.

Retired FBI agent Himmelsbach spent about a decade investigating the NORJAK case. He believes Cooper died during his jump but would like to know for sure. Himmelsbach is especially concerned with the folk hero status some people give to Cooper.

"I think he was just simply a sleazy, rotten criminal who was middle-aged, and his life had gone nowhere and he thought what a good idea and he might give it a try," Himmelsbach said.

On December 31, 2007, the FBI revived the case. Information on an FBI Web site shows the composite sketch of Cooper and photographs of the tie and tie tack he wore, recovered ransom bills, and the parachutes and canvas bag he left behind. All these years after the hijacking, people are still trying to figure out who D.B. Cooper really was and what happened to him.

"I think it's a great mystery," FBI agent Carr said. "What happened to this guy? The last thing we knew is he had $200,000 and bailed out of the

HIMMELSBACH ON THE HUNT

The FBI's Ralph Himmelsbach was the lead agent in the search for Cooper for eight years. He wrote *NORJAK: The Investigation of D.B. Cooper,* a book about his experiences hunting for the infamous hijacker. Himmelsbach believes that Cooper probably had a criminal record, received military training, and was familiar with the Pacific Northwest.

What is Himmelsbach's theory about the unsolved case? He believes Cooper probably died. "The night it happened, I thought he had a 50 percent chance [of surviving]," Himmelsbach said. "It has gone down since then."

back of a 727 November 24, 1971, and then from there we don't know."

In recent years scientists have continued to study the area where Brian Ingram found the three stacks of ransom money 30 years ago. They've studied the Little Washougal River and the Washougal River, which empty into the Columbia River. Did the ransom money first land in either of these rivers and then make its way into the Columbia? Did the rest of the money continue down the Columbia toward the Pacific Ocean? Could Cooper's body have traveled the same route?

"You know, the whole goal is to start bringing some science, some new technology, into the case," Carr said. "The investigation's long over. We know what we know from what the FBI has done all those years. And now it's time to, you know, maybe give someone else a chance, to allocate, or let someone else allocate their own resources to the investigation. And hopefully that shakes something new."

Who was D.B. Cooper, and what happened to him? It is unlikely we will ever know for certain. But people are still trying to solve the mystery.

On February 13, 1980, FBI agents used a backhoe, rakes, and screens to carefully sift through the sand along the Columbia River near Vancouver, Washington. They were searching the area where Brian Ingram had found some of the money from the Cooper hijacking.

TIMELINE

1964
Northwest Orient Airlines buys its first Boeing 727, which can take off at low speeds and land at small airports. At the time it is the only jet equipped with back stairs.

November 24
1971
A passenger who called himself Dan Cooper, hijacks Northwest Orient Airlines Flight 305 on its way to the Seattle-Tacoma airport. He demands $200,000 in $20 bills and four parachutes. He jumps from the plane's back stairs and is never seen or heard from again.

December 8
1971
Serial numbers of the Cooper money are released to the public. No one comes forward with any of the ransom loot.

April 7

1972

Richard Floyd McCoy hijacks United Airlines Flight 885. He demands $500,000 and four parachutes. Like Cooper, he parachutes from the rear stairs of the Boeing 727. Later captured, tried, and imprisoned, McCoy seems a likely suspect in the Cooper caper.

1974

The first D.B. Cooper Party is held in Ariel, Washington. The party becomes an annual affair, with Cooper look-alike contests and lots of storytelling.

1977

William Pratt Gossett is said to confess to a Salt Lake City, Utah, judge that he had been involved in a hijacking and might have left fingerprints behind. Gossett had told his son Greg that he was the NORJAK hijacker.

TIMELINE

1977 Ron and Pat Forman meet small-plane enthusiast Barbara Dayton, who claims that she disguised herself as a man and hijacked the Northwest Orient 727.

February 1980 An 8-year-old boy, Brian Ingram, finds $5,800 in decaying $20 bills on the shore of the Columbia River near Vancouver, Washington. Serial numbers match some in the Cooper case.

1981 The movie *The Pursuit of D.B. Cooper* opens. To get publicity for the film, Universal Pictures offers a $1 million reward for information leading to the arrest and conviction of D.B. Cooper. No one claims the reward, and the offer is eventually dropped.

1996 The Boeing 727 airplane that Cooper hijacked is scrapped in a Tennessee junkyard.

July 24

2000

An article in *U.S. News and World Report* magazine reveals that Duane L. Weber made a deathbed confession admitting he was D.B. Cooper.

2007

Lyle Christiansen, watching a TV episode of *Unsolved Mysteries*, sees the composite sketch of D.B. Cooper. He contacts the FBI, saying his brother, Kenneth Christiansen, had looked exactly like the Cooper sketch. He is certain his brother, now dead, was D.B. Cooper.

2010

FBI Special Agent Larry Carr says there is still a chance the NORJAK case can be solved. Although the hunt for Cooper is no longer active, the case remains open.

GLOSSARY

accomplice—someone who helps another person commit a crime

aerodynamic—designed to move through the air easily and quickly

aft—at or close to the back of an airplane, boat, or ship

circumstantial evidence—evidence in court that must be combined with reasoning to prove that a defendant is guilty

civilian—someone who is not a member of the police or armed forces

cockpit—area at the front of a plane where the pilot sits

composite sketch—drawing of a person that is created from eyewitness descriptions

dredge—to scrape sand, rocks, and mud from the bottom of a body of water

hijack—to take control of an airplane or other vehicle by force

microfilm—film on which printed materials are photographed at greatly reduced size for ease of storage

NORJAK—FBI's name for the 1971 case of the hijacking of Northwest Orient Flight 305

paratrooper—soldier trained to jump by parachute into battle

plummet—to fall straight down

ripcord—cord pulled to release a parachute

serial number—number that identifies something, such as a vehicle, appliance, or dollar bill

tie tack—pin with a receiving button or clasp that holds the two ends of a necktie together or holds the necktie to a shirt

ADDITIONAL RESOURCES

READ MORE

Grant, Walter. *D.B. Cooper, Where Are You: My Own Story.* Anchorage, Alaska: Publication Consultants, 2008.

Gunther, Max. *D.B. Cooper: What Really Happened?* Chicago: Contemporary Books, 1985.

Himmelsbach, Ralph P. *NORJAK: The Investigation of D.B. Cooper.* West Linn, Ore.: Norjak Project, 1986.

Rhodes, Bernie. *D.B. Cooper: The Real McCoy.* Salt Lake City: University of Utah Press, 1991.

Tosaw, Richard Thomas. *D.B. Cooper: Dead or Alive.* Ceres, Calif.: Tosaw Pub. Co., 1984.

INTERNET SITES

Use FactHound to find Internet sites related to this book. All of the sites on FactHound have been researched by our staff.

Here's all you do:
Visit *www.facthound.com*
Type in this code: 9780756543594

SELECT BIBLIOGRAPHY

Blevins, Robert. "Was Ken Christiansen of Northwest Airlines the REAL 'D.B. Cooper'?" Newsvine.com. 10 Oct. 2009. 31 March 2010. adventurebooks.newsvine.com/_news/2009/10/10/3262162-was-ken-christiansen-of-northwest-airlines-the-real-db-cooper-geoffrey-grey-of-the-new-york-magazine-says-yes-

Blumenthal, Les. "Citizen Sleuths Follow Trail of Elusive Hijacker D.B. Cooper." McClatchy Newspapers. 20 April 2009. 9 April 2010. www.mcclatchydc.com/homepage/story/66427.html

Coreno, Catherine. "D.B. Cooper: A Timeline." *New York Magazine*. 21 Oct. 2007. 31 March 2010. nymag.com/news/features/39617

Craig, John S. "D.B. Cooper Suspect Named: William Pratt Gossett." 31 May 2008. 9 April 2010. www.associatedcontent.com/article/796139/db_cooper_suspect_named_william_pratt.html?cat=17

"D.B. Cooper Party." 31 March 2010. www.2camels.com/d-b-cooper-party.php

Federal Bureau of Investigation. "D.B. Cooper Redux." 31 March 2010. www.fbi.gov/page2/dec07/dbcooper123107.html

Federal Bureau of Investigation. "Famous Cases: Richard Floyd McCoy, Jr.—Aircraft Hijacking." 31 March 2010. www.fbi.gov/libref/historic/famcases/mccoy/mccoy.htm

Gray, Geoffrey. "Unmasking D.B. Cooper." *New York Magazine*. 21 Oct. 2007. 31 March 2010. nymag.com/news/features/39593/

Joltin, Stephen. "D.B. Cooper Money: Ransom Money Is Being Auctioned on eBay." 10 June 2008. 9 April 2010. www.associated content.com/article/812643/d_b_cooper_money_ransom_ money_is_being.html?cat=7

KATU staff. "FBI: Comic Book Holds Clue in D.B. Cooper Case." 17 March 2009. 9 April 2010. www.komonews.com/news/ local/41406022.html

Krajicek, David. "DB Cooper The Legendary Daredevil." TruTV. 31 March 2010. www.trutv.com/library/crime/criminal_mind/ scams/DB_Cooper/

Pasternak, Douglas. "Mysteries of History: Skyjacker at Large." *U.S. News* Online. 24 July 2000. 31 March 2010. www.usnews. com/usnews/doubleissue/mysteries/cooper.htm

Seven, Richard. "D.B. Cooper: Perfect crime or perfect folly?" *Seattle Times.* 17 Nov. 1996. 31 March 2010. home.earthlink. net/~quade/dbcooper.html

Skolnik, Sam. "30 years ago, D.B. Cooper's night leap began a legend." *Seattle Post-Intelligencer.* 22 Nov. 2001. 31 March 2010. www.seattlepi.com/local/47793_vanished22.shtml

INDEX

ABOUT THE AUTHOR

Kay Melchisedech Olson is a longtime author and editor. She lives and writes in Minnesota.